MCO P4030.36A
LPP-2
16 Aug 94

MARINE CORPS ORDER P4030.36A

From: Commandant of the Marine Corps
To: Distribution List

Subj: MARINE CORPS PACKAGING MANUAL

Encl: (1) LOCATOR SHEET

1. <u>Purpose</u>. To provide instructions pertaining to the preservation, packing, unitization, and marking of Marine Corps material.

2. <u>Cancellation</u>. MCO P4030.36.

3. <u>Summary of Revision</u>. This revision contains a substantial number of changes and should be reviewed in its entirety.

4. <u>Action</u>. The procedures outlined in this Manual are to be implemented as soon as possible.

5. <u>Recommendation</u>. Recommendations concerning the contents of the Marine Corps Packaging Manual are invited. Such recommendations are to be forwarded to the Commandant of the Marine Corps (LPP-2) via the appropriate chain of command.

6. <u>Reserve Applicability</u>. This Manual is applicable to the Marine Corps Reserve.

7. <u>Certification</u>. Reviewed and approved this date.

J. A. BRABHAM
Deputy Chief of Staff
for Installations and Logis

DISTRIBUTION: PCN 10204130300

Copy to: 7000110 (55)
          7000160, 161, 166, 176 (4
          8145005 (2)
          700099, 144/8145001 (1)

DISTRIBUTION STATEMENT A: Approved for public release; distribution is unlimited.

LOCATOR SHEET

Subj: MARINE CORPS PACKAGING MANUAL

Location:_____
          (Indicate the location(s) of the copy(ies) of this
          Manual.)

MARINE CORPS PACKAGING MANUAL

RECORD OF CHANGES

Log completed change action, as indicated.

Change Number	Date of Change	Date Entered	Signature of Person Entering Change

MARINE CORPS PACKAGING MANUAL

CONTENTS

MARINE CORPS PACKAGING MANUAL

CHAPTER 1

GENERAL INFORMATION

MARINE CORPS PACKAGING MANUAL

CHAPTER 1

GENERAL INFORMATION

1000. PURPOSE. This Manual contains information on packaging
management and administration. It is intended as a tool in
improving packaging administration by delineating responsibilities
for packaging and promulgating basic operational guidance. As a
general summary, this Manual:

1. Implements Department of Defense (DoD) policy for preservation,
packing, unitization, and marking of materiel.

2. Provides guidance for selection and application of levels of
protection for varying conditions of supply, to include use of
commercial packaging.

3. Delineates packaging responsibilities for organizations whose
mission involves or interfaces with packaging.

4. Sets forth basic guidance for the establishment and operation
of packaging facilities.

5. Includes guidance for packaging surveillance and represervation
of material on which the original protection is maturing or has
deteriorated.

6. Provides guidance concerning availability, preparation, and use
of technical packaging data.

7. Gives criteria for field expediencies for accomplishing
protection for materiel in retrograde movement.

8. Provides basic guidance concerning proper utilization of
reusable containers.

9. Provides guidance concerning materials and techniques for
protection of secondary reparable items.

10. Provides guidance for protection of Marine Corps-sponsored
international logistics (IL) shipments.

11. Provides guidance for the adoption/utilization of modernized
techniques/current state-of-the-art in preservation and packing
operations.

12. Provides information concerning established channels for
research and exploratory development.

13. Contains information concerning formal and local training in packaging applicable to both military and civilian occupational specialties.

1001. <u>SCOPE</u>. The policies, criteria, and guidance set forth herein are applicable to all packaging of Marine Corps material. The scope of Marine Corps packaging encompasses the life cycle of the material from development and attainment of requisite protection at time of procurement, cyclic preservation maintenance of material during term of storage, preparation for shipment to using organizations, and the retrograde movement of serviceable and unserviceable reparable assets. Regulations, standards, handbooks, and specifications referenced in this Manual are listed in chapter 10.

MARINE CORPS PACKAGING MANUAL

CHAPTER 2

POLICIES FOR PRESERVATION, PACKING, UNITIZATION, AND MARKING

MARINE CORPS PACKAGING MANUAL

CHAPTER 2

POLICIES FOR PRESERVATION, PACKING, UNITIZATION, AND MARKING

SECTION 1:   GENERAL PACKAGING TERMS

2100. <u>PURPOSE</u>

1. This chapter implements DoD policy for packaging and supplements the joint DoD component policies promulgated in MCO 4030.33.

2. Uniform criteria is established for the selection and application of packaging at the time of procurement, accomplishment of protection prior to and during storage, and shipment among Marine Corps activities or to other requisitioners.

3. These policies and objectives apply to all Marine Corps activities whose mission involves any responsibility for protection of material throughout its life cycle and, specifically, from its development/acquisition until ultimate use or disposal.

2101. <u>EXPLANATION OF TERMS</u>. The following functional terms are applicable for the purpose of this Manual (also see MCO 4030.33):

1. <u>Containerization</u>. The use of an article of transport equipment designed to facilitate and optimize the movement of goods by one or more modes of transportation without intermediate handling of the contents (also see MCO P4600.7)

2. <u>Cyclic Preservation</u>. The represervation of materiel in storage on which previously applied protective measures have subsequently aged or deteriorated to a state requiring renewal of the initial protection.

3. <u>Exercising</u>. The exercising of equipment to redistribute preservative oils and lubricants.

    a. <u>Method I</u>. By self-contained power supply.

    b. <u>Method II</u>. By remote or external power source.

4. <u>Exterior Pack</u>. A container, bundle, or assembly which is sufficient by reason of design and construction to protect materiel during shipment and storage. This can be a unit pack or a container with any combination of unit or intermediate packs.

5. <u>Commercial Packaging</u>. The packaging materials and methods used by the supplier which meet the requirements of the distribution systems serving both DoD and industrial consumers.

6. <u>Intermediate Pack</u>. A wrap, box, or bundle which contains two or more unit packs of identical items.

7. <u>Marking</u>. Application of numbers, letters, labels, tags, symbols, or colors for handling and/or identification during shipment and storage.

8. <u>Military Packaging</u>. The materials and methods prescribed in Federal and military specifications, standards, drawings, or other authorized documents designed to provide the level of protection to prevent damage or deterioration during shipment, handling, and storage of material.

9. <u>Packaging</u>. A "generic" term covering all the processes and procedures used to protect materiel from deterioration and/or damage. This includes cleaning, drying, preserving, packing, unitization, and marking.

10. <u>Packing</u>. Assembly of items into a unit, intermediate, or exterior pack with necessary blocking, bracing, cushioning, weatherproofing, reinforcement, and marking.

11. <u>Preservation</u>. Application of protective measures including cleaning, drying, preservative materials, barrier materials, cushioning, and containers, as required.

12. <u>Unitization</u>. Assembly of packs of one or more line items of supply into a single load in such a manner that the load can be handled as a unit through the distribution system. Unitization (unitized loads/unit loads) encompasses consolidation in a container, placement on a pallet or load base, or securely binding together.

13. <u>Unit Pack</u>. The first tie, wrap, or container applied to a single item or a quantity thereof, or to a group of items of a single national stock number (NSN), preserved or unpreserved, which constitutes a complete or identifiable package.

14. <u>Reusable Containers</u>. A shipping and storage container that is designed for reuse without impairment of its protective function and can be repaired and/or refitted to prolong its life or to adapt it for shipment of items other than that for which it was originally intended. Reusable containers are either specialized or general purpose.

    a. Specialized reusable containers are uniquely configured to support and protect a specific item, or variety of items,

while in transportation, storage, and handling. A specialized
reusable container has an expected service life equal to or greater
than the service life of the item it is designed to protect.
Engineering drawings or equivalent are used to define form, fit,
function, materials, tolerances, and manufacturing techniques.
These containers are accountable in accordance with established
inventory management and accounting procedures.

   b. General purpose reusable containers are designed to
accommodate a number of different items within certain limits of
size, weight, and fragility. A general purpose reusable container
can be reused a limited number of times and may be identified by
military or Federal specifications.

MARINE CORPS PACKAGING MANUAL

CHAPTER 2

POLICIES FOR PRESERVATION, PACKING, UNITIZATION, AND MARKING

SECTION 2: PACKAGING POLICY

2200. <u>GENERAL POLICIES</u>

1. All Marine Corps materiel shall be afforded packaging protection adequate to prevent corrosion, deterioration, and physical damage during storage and distribution.

2. Maximum use will be made of commercial packaging in acquisition/procurement actions when such packaging satisfies Marine Corps needs (also see chapter 3).

3. Military levels of protection, "A," "B," and "C" (technical requirements) (see paragraph 2202), will be developed for all Marine Corps-managed items by the organizational element having responsibility for managing the packaging data segment of the Marine Corps Supply System. Technical requirements for each applicable level will satisfy storage and logistical conditions described in this chapter and will be documented in the manner prescribed under the DoD Standardization Program.

4. Packaging design will comply with requirements for the minimization of weight and cube (see MCO 4610.14), for size standardization (see MIL-STD-1187), and for efficiency of movement through the various modes of the transportation system.

5. Packaging prescriptions will include, as appropriate to the commodity and its usage, the prescribed quantity of the item to be included in the unit, intermediate and exterior pack, and unitized load.

6. Packaging requirements developed and prescribed for inclusion in specifications, standards, and contractual documents will provide the requisite level of protection and will be described in sufficient detail to promote competitive procurement and small business considerations.

7. Specifications, standards, and other relative standardization documents prescribing packaging (for which the Marine Corps is the preparing activity) will be coordinated by the preparing activity with a representative cross-section of the applicable segments of industry, industrial associations, and technical societies (see DoD 4120.3-M)

8. Packaging protection necessary to ensure serviceability and prevent physical damage throughout the anticipated storage and

distribution cycle will be provided at the time of procurement, to the maximum extent practicable. This protection may be obtained from the prime contractor, subcontractor, packaging service contractor, or other such means available to the procuring office. In-house packaging facilities may be used for purposes of initial packaging of procured items only when the sources enumerated in the preceding are not available, industry cannot furnish the service within the required timeframe, or when such services are not economically advantageous.

9. Material originally protected to a level lower than that required for a particular shipment or storage condition will be repackaged if a higher level is needed to:

    a. Comply with levels of protection known to be required for designated shipments, special projects, transportation and handling conditions, and storage environment.

    b. Meet the specific level of protection specified by a requisitioner.

10. Packaging protection may be reduced for containerized shipments when the items are intended for immediate use, when the containerization medium is retained as a storage/issue facility, or when it is known that favorable storage will be provided upon receipt. Material previously packaged at a higher degree of protection will not be repackaged to meet this requirement.

11. In selecting levels of protection for ammunition, explosives, or other dangerous materials, nothing in the policies or procedures contained in this Manual will be construed as authorizing any compromise with established regulations or safety standards.

12. Hazardous cargo, including shipments from supply sources to a consolidation/containerization point (CCP) for onward movement, will be packed, marked, and certified per DoD 4500.32-R, volume I, chapter 4, section II.

13. Logistics application of automated marking and reading symbols (LOGMARS) bar coded labels will be used to mark interior packs, outer containers, and selected documentation (see MCO 4000.51) Contracts will include a clause identifying LOGMARS requirements per MIL-STD-1189 and MIL-STD-129.

14. Performance oriented packaging (POP) requirements will be in compliance with the following regulations which govern the international transport of dangerous goods:

    a. The United Nations (UN) "Orange Book" entitled, "Transport of Dangerous Goods."

b. The "International Civil Air Organization (ICAO) Technical Instructions for the Safe Transport of Dangerous Goods by Air".

c. The "International Maritime Dangerous Goods Code" (IMDG) - DoD activities or commercial vendors who develop packaging designs for dangerous goods will conduct the necessary tests and show compliance or certification by marking their packages with approved logo and certification numbers.

15. Electrostatic discharge sensitive (ESDS) items will be packaged with electrostatic discharge (ESD) protective materials. Packaging, handling, and storage requirements and procedures will be per the requirements of MIL-MDBK-263 and MIL-STD-1686. Staples should never be used as a closure method for ESD protective barrier material bags.

16. Marine air-ground task force (MAGTF)-deployed units dominant criteria for packaging will be that which is imposed by the end use/employment of packaged materiel versus those criteria imposed by lift or other constraints.

a. Break-bulk/palletized cargo will be maximized for assault echelon and airlifted elements of the MAGTF.

b. Containerization will be maximized for all other dry cargo.

c. Cargo documentation for MAGTF supplies will be accomplished using automated methods common to LOGMARS application to enhance visibility, location, tracking, and retrievability aspects. These automated procedures will be in addition to current manual methods, those imposed by commercial shippers, or those imposed by the Military Traffic Management Command (MTMC) for commercially lifted overland, sea, or air movements.

17. Marine Corps activities are encouraged to use advanced packaging techniques in conjunction with the purchasing of supplies and equipment. Information concerning the performance and reliability of advanced packaging techniques can normally be provided by the supplier/manufacturer, and a determination should be made that the material or technique meets the performance requirements of MIL-P-116. Approval for use of nonspecification material will be obtained from the Commandant of the Marine Corps (CMC) (LPP-2).

18. Awareness of and concern for human safety and environmental protection will be inherent in the planning and execution of all policies and procedures outlined in this Manual. Amplifying instructions may be found in MCO 5100.25, MCO 6280.8, and MCO P11000.8. The intent of State and local pollution abatement laws, regulations, criteria, and standards also apply.

2201. OBJECTIVES

1. Promote uniformity in the development/selection and application
of packaging requirements for the same or similar items and,
likewise, for the same or similar conditions of storage and
distribution.

2. Ensure optimum life, utility, and performance of materiel
through prevention of corrosion, deterioration, or damage.

3. Facilitate efficient receipt, storage, inventory, and
distribution of materiel.

4. Assure essential and effective markings for identification and
handling throughout the storage and distribution cycles.

5. Effect economies by utilizing unit, intermediate, and exterior
packs which will result in the lowest overall cost.

6. Provide quality packaging that will enhance the materiel
readiness of the Marine Corps.

7. Ensure that requirements for packaging, cited in contracts
for procurement of materiel, are in consonance with policies stated
herein.

8. Provide for adequate occupational safety, health, and
environmental measures in packaging operations.

9. Promote maximum practicable use of industrial/commercial
packaging.

10. Promote utilization of packaging materials and containers that
are known to be reusable, or have reuse potential, and which have
minimum adverse impact on the ecology.

2202.   LEVELS OF PROTECTION

1. Military levels of protection are described in terms of the
performance expected of the package or pack, and must be translated
into specific technical or design requirements for individual items
or categories of items.

2. Levels of protection (technical requirements) for individual
items or categories of items are normally contained in
MIL-STD-2073-1, the commodity specification (section 5), or the
packaging specification applicable to a given category of items
(electronics, wheeled vehicles, handtools, etc.) -

3. The level of protection to be specified in procurement documents, or applied by Marine Corps activities, is dependent upon known factors of use, storage, and/or shipping. The technical requirements of the levels for either procurement or packaging facility application will normally be selected from documentation indicated in paragraph 2202.2, preceding.

4. The following are levels of protection for preservation and packing (see MCO 4030.33):

   a. Levels of Preservation

      (1) Level A. Preservation designed to protect an item of supply during shipment, handling, storage, and distribution to consignees worldwide.

      (2) Level B. Preservation designed to the unique requirements of selected commodities for which the deprocessing demands of Level A preservation (would) bear significantly on the operational readiness of the item; e.g., vehicles and weapons.

      (3) Level C. Minimal preservation designed to protect an item for single trip transport and immediate use.

   b. Levels of Packing

      (1) Level A. Maximum protection to meet the most severe worldwide shipment, handling, and storage conditions. A Level A pack must, in tandem with the applied preservation, be capable of protecting materiel from the effects of direct exposure to extremes of climate, terrain, and operational and transportation environments. Examples of situations which indicate a need for use of Level A pack are mobilization (strategic and theater deployment and employment), open storage, and deck loading. Examples of containers used to meet the Level A requirements are overseas-type wood boxes; and fiberglass, plastic, and metal reusable containers.

      (2) Level B. Intermediate protection to meet moderate worldwide shipment, handling, and storage conditions. A Level B pack, in tandem with the applied preservation, must be capable of protecting material not directly exposed to the extremes of climate, terrain, and operational and transportation environments. Examples of situations which indicate a need for a Level B pack are security assistance, selected containerized overseas shipments, and anticipated favorable conditions. Examples of containers used to meet the Level B pack requirements are domestic wood crates, weather-resistant fiberboard containers, fast-pack containers, weather-resistant fiber drums, and weather-resistant paper and multi-wall shipping sacks.

(3) <u>Level C</u>. Minimum protection to meet conditions of a favorable logistics path. The Level C pack will, in tandem with the applied preservation, protect materiel against effects sustainable within the Continental United States (CONUS) transportation system or outside of CONUS (OCONUS) shipments by air for immediate use. Examples of situations which indicate use of a Level C pack are CONUS and OCONUS shipments to fill high priority requisitions, shipments of mission stock to CONUS inventory, small parcel shipments, and direct vendor deliveries. Examples of containers used for Level C packs include domestic grade fiberboard boxes, domestic multi-wall shipping sacks, and small parcel mailing envelopes.

2203. <u>COMMERCIAL PACKAGING</u>. Commercial packaging will be acceptable for any level of protection whenever the technical design details of the package meet all conditions of the level of protection specified. Commercial packaging must provide the same level of protection against physical and environmental damage as the military package. It will be marked to the level of protection to which it complies.

1. Items will be given the degree of protection normally employed by the supplier to afford protection against corrosion, deterioration, and damage during shipment.

2. Protection will be that used for distribution directly to a using customer or for subsequent redistribution, as required.

3. Wholesale assembly bulk-type packaging practices, such as used in interplant and intraplant shipments to jobbers, are not acceptable unless they are the usual trade practices for selected commodities.

4. The technical requirements will be incorporated in standardization and acquisition documents, as applicable.

5. Specific industry standards such as Electronic Industries Association or Aerospace Industries Association Standards may be used, where appropriate.

6. American Society for Testing and Materials (ASTM) D 3951 is an acceptable reference document for commercial packaging. Well defined individual company standards meeting the minimum requirements of ASTM D3951 may also be used.

2204. <u>SELECTION AND APPLICATION OF MILITARY LEVELS OF PROTECTION AND COMMERCIAL PACKAGING.</u> Determinations to use appropriate military levels of protection (or commercial packaging) will be governed by knowledge of conditions of shipment, class of materiel, and duration of storage. The nature and characteristics of an item and its susceptibility to corrosion, deterioration, and physical damage are also essential factors for consideration and will be the basis for determining the method of unit preservation. Levels of protection apply equally to the preservation and packing functions. Criteria (partial) applicable to the levels of military packaging (and for commercial packaging) are as follows (also see MCO 4030.33):

1. Level A

    a. High dollar value items having critical characteristics where corrosion or physical damage cannot be risked.

    b. Principal end items and secondary technical items:

        (1) Placed in outdoor storage.

        (2) Likely to be exposed to the environment.

        (3) Likely to be exposed to multiple or severe handling in shipment or storage.

    c. Items not necessarily of high dollar value but critical in nature, application, or requirement where any degree of corrosion, deterioration, or physical damage would render the items unserviceable or unusable.

2. Level B

    a. General stocks (other than those indicated in the preceding) for CONUS warehouse storage and for redistribution upon demand and under favorable shipping conditions.

    b. Overseas containerized shipments, or other favorable shipment modes, where extended environmental exposure is not anticipated.

3. Level C

    a. Assets acquired under the direct support stock control (DSSC) subsystem.

    b. Repair parts to support depot maintenance activities.

    c. Deliveries for first destination consumption, to include possible short-term warehouse storage.

    d. Deliveries for first destination use, to include possible extended storage in controlled humidity space.

    e. Containerized shipments (transit exposure not likely to occur).

4. <u>Commercial Packaging</u>

    a. Commercial packaging may be adequate/used to satisfy any level of protection. This decision of adequacy can be based upon qualified knowledge of a given industry/supplier's packaging practices, or upon an analysis of the technical design details (materials and workmanship) of the industry package to meet the logistical conditions.

    b. After due consideration of the criteria in paragraph 2204.4a, preceding, commercial packaging is normally suitable for distribution directly to a using customer.

2205.   PACKAGING OF FOREIGN MILITARY SALES AND MILITARY ASSISTANCE PROGRAM (MAP) MATERIEL

1. All foreign military sales (FMS) and MAP materiel will be afforded Level A protection, since export shipment is generally by ocean vessel and may be subject to exposure and multiple handling during transit. This policy is established to assure safe delivery of material to the purchasing country in a serviceable condition.

2. Exceptions to this policy would be in consideration of the following shipment modes and logistical conditions:

    a. Air shipment (from origin to destination), Level B.

    b. Parcel post/consolidations (at point of origin), Level B.

    c. Shipment for known immediate use, Level B.

    d. Known favorable storage, transportation, and handling conditions (e.g., containerized), Level B.

    e. At the request of the receiving country.

3. Material in stores already packaged to Level A requirements will not be repackaged to meet the exception criteria cited in paragraph 2205.2, preceding. Materiel already Level A unit packaged will be shipped without impairing the quality of protection originally afforded.

4. Containers for Level A protection of FMS/MAP shipments will be other than fiberboard. Weather-resistant grades of fiberboard are suitable for Level B applications cited in paragraph 2205.2, preceding.

5. Commercial-type preservation may be used for FMS shipments when it is determined that such packaging (materials and workmanship) meets the requirements specified for Level A protection (see paragraph 2204.4a).

MARINE CORPS PACKAGING MANUAL

CHAPTER 3

PACKAGING RESPONSIBILITIES

MARINE CORPS PACKAGING MANUAL

CHAPTER 3

PACKAGING RESPONSIBILITIES

3000. <u>GENERAL</u>. Several organizational elements share in the responsibility of providing and maintaining adequate protection (life cycle) for materiel acquired for the Marine Corps Supply System. These organizational elements include item management, procurement, maintenance, warehousing, and distribution.

3001. <u>POLICY AND PROGRAM MANAGEMENT</u>. The CMC (LPP-2) is the office of primary responsibility for management and administration of packaging throughout the Marine Corps. The CMC (LPP-2):

1. Participates with major DoD components in the development and implementation of DOD/joint service packaging policies.

2. Promulgates policies and level of protection selection and application criteria for adequate, economical life-cycle protection for all Marine Corps Supply System materiel.

3. Provides guidance/direction to other headquarters agencies and field activities whose missions involve or interface with packaging. This responsibility may be concerned with:

   a. Coordination/review of "preparation for delivery requirements" contained or developed for inclusion in such documents as Federal and/or military specifications and standards, procurement documents, integrated logistics support plans, and statements of work to ensure compliance with policy and objectives.

   b. Providing general guidance to and surveillance over packaging operations administered at the various field activities, both within the supporting establishment and the Fleet Marine Forces (FMF), and providing for technical and operational assistance, as required.

4. Maintains necessary liaison with other DoD components, Federal Government agencies, and industry on matters of packaging technology.

5. Plans for conferences and staff visits, as deemed necessary, to promote effective, efficient packaging programs.

6. Coordinates packaging innovations (and packaging improvement requests) which are of interest to more than one Marine Corps activity.

7. Provides the sponsor for the military occupational field for Packaging Specialist 3052 and is responsible for maintaining the military occupational specialty (MOS) description, as required, in developing MOS utilization and assignment criteria.

8. Provides for Marine Corps membership/liaison representation for DoD, the Defense Packaging Policy Group (DPPG), joint service boards, committees, and working groups.

9. Provides the chairperson for the Marine Corps Preservation, Packaging, and Packing (P3) Committee; directs the activities of the P3 committee or any task groups; and reports to Marine Corps planners, programmers, and decisionmakers the results of committee actions (see MCO 5420.17).

10. Participates in determining requirements for and coordinates establishing. packaging training programs, in cooperation with cognizant training agencies internal and external to the Marine Corps.

11. Serves as the "focal point" for special actions or major packaging problems, when either is considered to be of broad impact.

3002. **PACKAGING DATA MANAGEMENT**. The Commander, Marine Corps Logistics Bases (COMMARCORLOGBASES), (Code 87), Albany, Georgia, is the office of primary responsibility for the collection, storage, maintenance, and distribution of packaging data. The COMMARCORLOGBASES (Code 87) develops a data base of Defense Integrated Data System (DIDS) data elements and Marine Corps specific data elements, compatible with the requirements of MIL-STD-1388, MIL-STD-2073-1, and MIL-STD-2073-2. Major functions are as follows:

1. <u>Data Base Maintenance</u>. Data base maintenance functions are used to maintain the integrity of the technical data and data base.

2. <u>Data Base Inquiry</u>. Data base inquiry functions are used to search and interrogate the technical data to provide information to build management review reports and to provide on-line query of technical data files.

3. <u>Data Transfer</u>. Data transfer functions are used to transfer extracted data between systems for update and review.

3003. ITEM MANAGER RESPONSIBILITIES. Organizations having responsibility for acquisition/acquisition sponsorship of major end items, systems, secondary technical items, and general supplies and equipment will coordinate with the packaging data base manager to ensure:

1. Development of adequate technical packaging requirements in conjunction with major items/systems design and development. Contractor-developed packaging data will be concurred in by the item manager/sponsor agency and produced in the prescribed format of a specification, drawing, or data sheet for standardized usage.

2. Adequate protection for materiel entering the supply system at the time of procurement, to the extent practicable (see chapter 2). The required military level of protection will be incorporated in procurement actions by detailed packaging prescription or by reference to packaging documents listed in the DoD Index of Specifications and standards (DODISS).

    a. In the interest of economy, levels of protection prescribed for application at the time of procurement shall be the minimum packaging required to afford adequate protection for the type of items and the anticipated conditions of storage and shipment (see chapter 2).

    b. Commercial packaging of the type utilized in normal retail distribution practices shall be used to the maximum extent practicable, when such will satisfy the logistical requirements of the supply system (see chapter 2 for detailed criteria).

3004. <u>STORAGE AND DISTRIBUTION ACTIVITIES</u>

1. Activities, whose mission involves warehousing operations, also have the responsibility to effectively operate and maintain packaging facilities. Accordingly, maximum effort will be devoted to modernization/mechanization/automation0n of packaging facilities to achieve efficiency and overall economy of operations (see chapters 2 and 4 of this Manual and MCO 4450.10).

2. Specific/major responsibilities include the following:

    a. Provide adequate protection (prior to storage or further shipment) for materiel received when necessary protection was not or could not be provided at the source of procurement or supply.

    b. Maintain continuing quality protection during the term of storage in compliance with the care-in-storage program and chapter 5.

    c. Provide adequate protection for materiel selected for shipment to Marine Corps customers or other requisitioners.

d. Apply minimum adequate preservation measures to unserviceable materiel to maintain an "as is" condition pending repair or other disposition.

e. Acquire current packaging technical data on items for which there are recurring demands; i.e., up-to-date specifications, standards, preservation data sheets, drawings, etc., in hard copy, microfilm-microfiche, or a computerized data storage and retrieval system.

f. Make maximum practicable use of consolidation/unitization of material for shipment.

g. Investigate packaging innovations of Government or industry origin that may merit adoption for improvement of Marine Corps packaging. Refer proposals for official test and evaluation of new materials and techniques to the CMC (LPP-2) for appropriate action (see MCO 4030.34)

h. Participate in the DoD Packaging Improvement Program, utilizing SF 364 (Report of Discrepancy (ROD)) to report all material that is received damaged or inadequately prepared for storage or shipment (including excessive packaging) per the requirements of SECNAVINST 4355.18.

i. Provide required packaging in support of depot maintenance repair/rebuild of items prior to return to customer activities or to storage.

3005. FLEET MARINE FORCE ORGANIZATIONS

1. An intermediate capability for packaging is required at the Force Service Support Group (FSSG) level to accomplish preservation and packing for reparable assets. During in-garrison periods, the base facility is under the operational control of the tenant FSSG, thus rendering the FSSG self-sufficient. This capability is essential in providing:

a. Support for the receipt and issue of materiel, to include repacking to satisfy quantitative/unit of issue requirements of FMF units.

b. Accomplishing the normal care-in-storage program, renewing protection that is maturing or has already deteriorated.

c. Performing the preparation of retrograde material being evacuated to maintenance facilities and serviceable material being returned to stock.

   d.   Satisfying requirements for packaging generated by
deployments/maneuvers/training exercises.

   e.   Ensuring the readiness of prepositioned war reserve stocks
(PWRS).

   f.   On-the-job training (OJT) of MOS 3052 Marines.

2.   In the absence of an established base-type facility, minimal
capability for packaging can be provided by utilizing field
expedients; i.e., improvised methods. Guidelines for field
expediencies are set forth in chapter 9 of this Manual and
chapter 5 of MCO P4030.23D.

3006. <u>FIELD UNITS AND RESERVE ORGANIZATIONS.</u> Field units of the
FMF's and Reserve organizations will provide a minimum degree of
protection for reparable assets for retrograde shipment to the
appropriate maintenance or storage activity. Packaging
expediencies for activities lacking adequate facilities are set
forth in chapter 9 of this Manual and chapter 5 of MCO P4030.23D.

MARINE CORPS PACKAGING MANUAL

CHAPTER 4

PACKAGING FACILITIES AND BASIC OPERATING PROCEDURES

MARINE CORPS PACKAGING MANUAL

MARINE CORPS PACKAGING MANUAL

CHAPTER 4

PACKAGING FACILITIES AND BASIC OPERATING PROCEDURES

SECTION 1: PACKAGING FACILITIES

4100. <u>GENERAL INFORMATION</u>. All Marine Corps activities involved in storage and distribution, or having custody of backup and contingency stocks, have a responsibility to accomplish military levels of protection and/or storage surveillance/represervation.

4101. <u>PACKAGING MACHINERY AND EQUIPMENT</u>

1. The types and capacities of machinery and equipment to adequately outfit a packaging installation will be governed by the primary mission of an activity and the volume of preservation and packing required to support storage and distribution activities. Activities whose mission assignment involves protection of high volume receipts from commercial procurement, all types of commodities, worldwide distribution, and high echelon and high volume of maintenance may require a broad range of packaging machinery and equipment. Conversely, activities whose mission concerns maintenance of protection levels previously applied, and/or protection for retrograde movements, may require the minimum of equipment and machinery. Likewise, activities concerned primarily with the preparation for shipment of clothing and textile items require the minimum of equipment.

2. The following are types of packaging operations:

    a. <u>Large-Scale Packaging Operations</u>. Packaging equipment for large-scale operations should be those that lend themselves to maximum practicable mechanization to facilitate work process flow, minimize manual handling, and promote efficiency. Examples of such equipment include, but are not limited to, the following:

        (1) Mechanized cleaning tanks.

        (2) Mechanized drying facilities.

        (3) Mechanized preservative tanks.

        (4) Automatic or semiautomatic packaging machines and bag and box makers.

        (5) Powered strapping, closing, and banding equipment.

        (6) Automated marking systems.

b. Small Volume Operations. When the volume of materiel
requiring preservation and packing is small, manual equipment of
the varieties indicated in paragraph 4101.2a, preceding, may be
adequate. However, mechanization of the cleaning and preservative
application functions is normally desirable for efficiency,
minimizing the potential for recontamination of cleaned items, and
disruption of preservative coatings.

4102. PACKAGING ORGANIZATION

1. To ensure maximum effectiveness, economy, and efficiency of
packaging facilities, it is imperative that a proper packaging
organization be instituted. Cleaning, drying, preservation, and
packing, while being separate and distinct functions, are
interdependent. Similarly, the level of preservation and the level
of packing impact upon each other (as indicated in chapter 2).
Therefore, the total packaging function(s) should be an integrated
operation comprised of all packaging functions; i.e., cleaning,
drying, preservation, packing, unitization, and marking.

2. Integrated packaging functions will prove to be more efficient
and economical to operate.

    a. Certain equipment required in preservation operations can
be used in packing operations as well and vice versa; e.g., box
making/box assembly equipment, container closing devices, and
marking equipment.

    b. Integrated packaging functions eliminate or minimize
duplicate prefabrication and prepositioning of containers and
consumable supplies, to include cushioning, blocking, and bracing.

3. Packaging expediencies for activities having occasional or
situational requirements to perform military packaging are set
forth in chapter 9.

4103. PRESERVATION FACILITIES. For the purpose of this Manual, a
preservation facility is an area(s) , covered or open, for
processing major items, such as vehicular equipment (self-propelled
and/or towed) and other large, heavy items which cannot be
accommodated on packaging lines discussed in paragraph 4102,
preceding. Equipment required to process such items consist of,
but are not limited to, the following:

1. Special devices to facilitate "preservative run-in" for
internal combustion engines.

2. Equipment to atomize spray preservatives into enclosed areas.

3.   Inspection equipment, such as boroscopes, for storage quality control purposes.

4.   Portable banding machinery and equipment.

5.   Special rigs (mobile preservation) to process equipment onsite at outside storage locations.

6.   Special equipment required for method II exercising of vehicles.

MARINE CORPS PACKAGING MANUAL

CHAPTER 4

POLICIES FOR PRESERVATION, PACKING, UNITIZATION, AND MARKING

SECTION 2: BASIC OPERATING PROCEDURES FOR MARINE CORPS PACKAGING
FACILITIES

4200. <u>GENERAL INFORMATION</u>. Packaging accomplished at Marine Corps
facilities will conform to the requirements of MIL-STD-2073-1,
MIL-STD-129, MIL-P-116, and any specific instruction issued by the
CMC (LPP-2) for particular items or circumstances.

4201. <u>OPERATIONAL GUIDANCE</u>

1. MIL-STD-2073-1 provides criteria for control and development of
standard requirements for like items based on physical
characteristics, chemical characteristics, fragility, dimensions,
and weight. This standard will be used in developing detailed
packaging requirements for application in contracts and as a
procedural document. This standard also supplements MIL-STD-1367.
MIL-STD-129 provides the requirements for the uniform marking of
military supplies and equipment for shipment and storage.
MIL-P-116 covers the fundamental requirements for cleaning and
drying, preservative materials (and their application), and basic
methods and submethods of protection. This broad range of methods
and submethods incorporates the use of a wide variety of materials
for the stages of packaging mentioned in the preceding. However,
in the interest of economy and efficiency of operations, concerted
effort will be devoted to standardization to the least number of
methods and materials adaptable to the greatest possible number of
items of the active inventory.

2. Operational guidance for accomplishing MIL-P-116 methods of
preservation is contained in MCO P4030.31. That directive
describes and illustrates the step-by-step process of unit and
intermediate preservation, and it cites the applicable
specifications for material and supplies required.

3. Operational guidance concerning external container selection,
fabrication, and application (packing) is contained in
MCO P4030.21. That directive complements MCO P4030.31 and the unit
protection provided by prescribing container applications suitable
for all modes of transportation and varying environments of
storage.

4202. PACKAGING DESIGN AND ENGINEERING

1. Unit and intermediate packages and exterior containers (packs) will be designed to displace the minimum weight and cube. In packaging design and engineering for all levels of protection, cognizance will be taken of item characteristics, requirements for handling, and storage conditions prior to use. Decisions concerning methods and materials to use will be based on the most critical feature of the item to be packaged. Army Materiel Command Pamphlet (AMCP) 706-121 (Packaging and Pack Engineering) sets forth fundamental policies and principles applicable to design and engineering to military levels and methods of packaging and is approved for Marine Corps use. Copies of AMCP 706-121 should be obtained through normal publication supply channels.

2. AMCP 706-121 also contains valuable information on packaging restrictions and limitations imposed by the distribution system. Additionally, it identifies Department of Transportation and carrier rules and regulations applicable to safety in handling and transportation of commodities.

4203. QUANTITY PACKAGING

1. Only items of the same NSN will be placed in the same unit and/or intermediate pack, except sets/kits.

2. The quantity per unit pack is an important factor affecting the effectiveness of the storage and issue process and, in many cases, the quality of materiel in storage. The quantity per unit pack is normally established by the item managing element. Ideally, the quantity package should be the smallest quantity normally distributed to the ultimate user, or the quantity of the item required in single applications. Unit quantities greater than those required under the aforementioned conditions result in unnecessary handling and repackaging costs, as well as deterioration of those items remaining in the opened pack.

3. The criteria set forth in chapter 2 will be followed in determining unit pack quantities.

4204. INTERMEDIATE PACKAGING. Intermediate packaging (packing of two or more identical unit packs into another interior container) may be desirable for small or lightweight packs. Intermediate packaging facilitates handling, storage, inventory, and issue operations. Intermediate packaging may also be used to complement the protection afforded by the unit pack, when warranted.

Intermediate packaging is recommended under the following circumstances (see MCO P4030.31 and MIL-P-14232)

1. Bagged items (unit pack), unless the materials and workmanship used in fabricating the bag meet the requirement of the exterior container for the level of protection specified.

2. Small bin size items.

3. Upgrading or supplementing the protection initially applied as unit preservation.

4205. <u>EXTERIOR CONTAINERS (FOR LEVEL A, B AND C SHIPMENTS)</u>

1. As a general rule, exterior container or individual packs, for shipment or storage, will contain items of the same NSN only (collateral equipment and consolidation/multipacks/transport containers are exceptions). The following factors will be considered when selecting an exterior container (also see MCO P4030.21)

   a. Level of protection required.

   b. Item characteristics; i.e., size, weight, configuration, vulnerability to damage from shock, vibration, etc.

   c. Type of load.

   d. Rigidity necessary to protect the load.

   e. Cost and availability of the selected container and the cost that such a container will save or generate.

   f. Ease of handling the loaded container.

   g. Storage and handling facilities available to the receiver.

   h. The requirement to keep tare weight and cube to the minimum.

2. To facilitate handling and storage (as a general rule) the gross weight of the contents and container will not exceed 250 pounds, except when the weight of a single item, components, or assemblies of collective-type items (with a single NSN) exceeds this limitation. In this case, the gross weight will be governed by the requirements of the applicable container specification or the guidance provided by MCO P4030.21.

3. Containers with a gross weight exceeding 250 pounds will be provided with skids to facilitate handling. Likewise, containers

weighing more than 100 pounds with length and width dimensions greater than 48 inches by 24 inches or any container which due to size or weight must be pushed, dragged, or handled by mechanical equipment should be provided with skids designed and spaced adequately to permit four-way entry/handling by forklift trucks.

4. Container selection charts, criteria for selecting containers, and guidance concerning fabrication and use of exterior containers are contained in MCO P4030.21 and AMCP 706-121. Blocking, bracing, and securing of items and packs within shipping containers shall conform to the requirements of MIL-STD-1186.

4206. REUSABLE CONTAINERS

1. Reusable containers will be used, to the maximum extent practicable, for the shipment of large, bulky, high dollar value items. The following guidelines (partial) will be used to determine when reusable containers are economical and logistically practicable:

    a. The container can serve a dual purpose as a shipping/storage unit.

    b. The cost of the container is offset through multiple reuse as compared to the cost of a single shipment disposal container.

    c. The item is designated as recoverable/reparable.

    d. The need exists for periodic inspection or exercising of the contained item.

2. Examples of items for which reusable containers may be suitable include:

    a. Missiles and missile components.

    b. Electronics units.

    c. Engines.

    d. Transmissions.

    e. Axle assemblies.

3. Additional criteria for the selection of reusable containers, special features of design, and application are contained in MCO P4030.21 and AMCP 706-121. Care must be exercised to assure that old markings (identification and address) are removed when reusing containers.

4207. <u>FIBERBOARD CONTAINERS</u>

1. Fiberboard containers, when used properly, afford excellent
opportunities for reduction in costs of preservation and packing,
as well as corresponding savings in other related areas of supply
distribution, particularly for domestic shipments. However, they
will not be used as exterior shipping containers for items
requiring Level A protection or when it is known or anticipated
that the shipment will be subjected to prolonged exposure during
transit, rough handling, or outdoor storage upon receipt. When
fiberboard containers are used as exterior shipping containers,
they will be marked to indicate Level B or C protection.

2. Fiberboard containers generally will not be used to pack
type III loads as defined in MCO P4030.21. However, the proper use
of scored pads, die cuts, and sleeves will convert many type III
loads to type II loads, thereby permitting their use.

3. More detailed instructions on the use of fiberboard containers
can be found in MCO P4030.21.

4208. <u>MULTIPACK/CONSOLIDATED SHIPMENTS</u>

1. Multipacks are exterior containers which are used to
consolidate assorted items for shipment to a single destination.
Multipack containers must meet the requirements for the levels of
protection specified. All items shipped within the multipack
containers will be given unit protection to the level of packaging
required for the anticipated conditions and will be properly
identified before being placed in the multipack containers.

2. Consolidated shipments, in the context of this Manual, refer to
transportation containerized shipments, such as SEAVAN, MILVAN,
QUADCON's, PALCON's, etc. Use of cargo containers is covered in
MCO P4600.7. It is considered that these units, due to their
construction, offer protection supplemental to that afforded by
normal packaging methods. The supplemental protection thus
provided will be duly regarded in determining whether military
levels of packing or use of the usual exterior containers can be
reduced or eliminated for materiel shipped therein. However, the
protection required for materiel during transit, or after removal
from the containerization media, will not be compromised.

4209. WEATHERPROOFING (CASE LINERS AND SHROUDS). In some
instances, weatherproofing of the final pack may be required to
prevent deterioration of both the contents and the packaging
materials used to provide unit and intermediate protection. When

extreme climatic conditions are involved, waterproof case liners
should be used to divert water and to protect against the entry of
dust, dirt, or other foreign matter. Detailed information on
weatherproofing or waterproofing, by use of container liners or
shrouds, is provided in MCO P4030.21.

4210. <u>CLOSURE AND STRAPPING (REINFORCING) OF CONTAINERS.</u> Closure
and strapping shall be in accordance with the requirements of the
applicable container specification.

4211. <u>BLOCKING, BRACING, AND CUSHIONING.</u> Blocking, bracing,
cushioning, and other measures used to immobilize items in
containers shall meet the requirements of MIL-STD-1186.
Operational guidance and approved procedures for blocking and
bracing are set forth in MCO P4030.21.

4212. <u>PACKAGING MATERIALS, SUPPLIES, AND EQUIPMENT.</u> Commonly used
cleaning, preservation, cushioning, packing, and marking materials
are listed in Marine Corps data lists for Federal Supply Groups 68,
80, and 81.

4213. <u>DANGEROUS/HAZARDOUS MATERIALS.</u> Materials classified as
"dangerous or hazardous" will be packed and labeled in accordance
with the applicable model regulations, DoD tests reports; or
special instructions issued by cognizant regulatory agencies.
MCO P4030.19 contains instructions for the preparation of
explosives and other dangerous materials for shipment by military
aircraft. Compliance with the requirements of MCO P4030.19 is
mandatory, and dangerous materials offered for shipment by military
aircraft require certification of compliance (DD Form 1387-2,
Special Handling Data/Shipping Paper Certification).

4214. <u>RADIOACTIVE MATERIAL.</u> Special handling, packaging, and
storage requirements may apply to items containing radioactive
material (refer to MCO P4400.105).

4215. <u>MARKING.</u> Each unit pack, intermediate pack, and shipping
container, including items which are stored and shipped unpacked,
will be marked per the requirements of MIL-STD-129 (see chapter 6
for more specific guidance).

4216. <u>SALVAGE REUSE, AND DISPOSAL OF PACKAGING MATERIAL.</u> In the
interest of economy and in keeping with the pollution abatement
provisions of MCO P11000.8, maximum reuse shall be made

of packaging materials, when technically and economically feasible.
Materials that lend themselves to salvage and reuse include
barriers, cushioning, fiberboard (boxes and material), and wooden
and metal containers. Likewise, applicable provisions of
MCO P11000.8 will be adhered to for recycling and disposal of
packaging materials

MARINE CORPS PACKAGING MANUAL

CHAPTER 5

PACKAGING MAINTENANCE (REPACKAGING)

MARINE CORPS PACKAGING MANUAL

CHAPTER 5

PACKAGING MAINTENANCE (REPACKAGING)

5000. **GENERAL INFORMATION**

1. Preserved and packed materiel are often held in the Marine Corps Supply System for long periods of time. The depth and diversity of supply system assets and the low turnover rate for many items present the potential that protected items can again become subject to corrosion, deterioration, and physical damage due to aging, decomposition of packaging materials applied, and container fatigue. Also, for major items, such as self-powered vehicles and equipment, the continuity of protection must be maintained by periodic exercising to redistribute preservative oils to critical surfaces in enclosed areas, such as crankcases, transmissions, differentials, etc. Therefore, an effective program of packaging maintenance is essential to ensure that the original or initial protection measures applied to items continue to provide the protection required to maintain item serviceability.

2. The packaging maintenance measures contained in this chapter are fundamental to the care and storage of supplies.

5001. **OBJECTIVE**. The primary objective of a packaging maintenance program is to maintain the serviceability of all stored materiel through effective preservation and packing measures. Specific efforts encompassed in this objective include:

1. Random sampling of materiel received through procurement action.

2. Inspecting serviceable assets in storage, or assets being returned to stores, to detect the presence of corrosion, deterioration, fungus growth, mildew, container fatigue, or any situation which presents the potential for the foregoing circumstances.

3. Inspecting unserviceable items awaiting repair to detect damage and/or prevent further corrosion or deterioration.

4. Periodic technical inspection and exercising of equipment for which the integrity of preservation is maintained by redistribution/recirculation of contained preservatives and lubricants.

5. Initiating corrective action when improper storage practices contribute to the corrosion, deterioration, or physical damage observed.

6. Correcting observed deficiencies on location, to the extent practicable. Such action may include container repairs, resealing of packages and containers, replacing broken or loose banding, correcting improper markings, and other similar actions which can be accomplished without removal to packaging facilities.

7. Operational test of major and secondary technical items, in conjunction with technical inspection and exercising, to ascertain satisfactory performance or condition prior to representation.

8. Renewing preservation and packing, as necessary.

5002. <u>PACKAGING DEFECTS</u>. For the purpose of care-in-storage, packaging defects are classified as follows:

1. Preservation, Packing, and Marking (Critical). A critical preservation, packing, or marking defect is a defect which judgment and experience indicate is likely to present a hazard to the safety of personnel or damage to other materiel in storage; e.g., improper preservation, packing, and marking of items classified as "dangerous or hazardous."

2. <u>Preservation Defect</u>

    a. Major. Inadequate preservation is a major defect if it has permitted or will permit any degree of corrosion or deterioration of a critical surface, or extensive corrosion or deterioration of a noncritical surface. In addition, inadequate preservation is a major defect if it fails to provide necessary protection against physical damage or if it will permit impairment of an item to render it unserviceable for use.

    b. Minor. Inadequate-preservation is a minor defect if it has permitted the onset of minimal corrosion or incipient deterioration of noncritical surfaces, providing the presence of such corrosion or deterioration would not adversely affect the operability or efficient utilization of an item. Preservation which is not in strict conformance with specification requirements but is deemed sufficient to afford necessary protection to the item is a minor defect.

3. <u>Packing Defect</u>

    a. <u>Major</u>. Inadequate packing is a major defect if it fails to provide necessary protection against physical damage or damage from environmental exposure during shipment, handling, and storage.

    b. <u>Minor</u>. Inadequate packing is a minor defect if it is not in strict accord with specifications but is sufficient to protect the item against physical damage.

4. <u>Marking Defect</u>

a. <u>Major</u>. Incorrect marking and/or a lack of identification, special, or precautionary markings is a major defect if it could result in the loss of or damage to the item.

b. <u>Minor</u>. Minor marking defects include incomplete or missing contractor's name or address, requisition number, weight, cube, or preservation information, provided that such defective marking would not result in damage to the item.

5003. <u>WORKLOAD.</u> The workload of packaging maintenance (reprocessing) is the direct result of actions required by program directives, such as the following:

1. MCO P4790.3, Marine Corps Integrated Maintenance Management System Depot Procedures Manual.

2. DoD 4145.19-R-1, Storage and Materials Handling.

5004. <u>GUIDELINES FOR REPROCESSING</u>

1. Preservation or reprocessing which may result from surveillance, inspection, exercising, and rebuild actions required by the foregoing programs may range from very minor work that can be performed on location, to complete preservation or represervation of major end items. Consistent with the policy set forth in chapter 2, preservation of items during the term of storage or incident to shipment will be the minimum necessary to assure adequate or continued protection. Excessive or unnecessary represervation will be avoided.

2. Normally, reprocessing resulting from care-in-storage inspections will be to the level of protection originally provided. However, in those instances where large quantities of a single line item require reprocessing1 effort should be made, through established supply/inventory management channels, to determine supply system requirements for the item to preclude expenditure of work-hours and funds on items which may be obsolete or in excess.

3. Criteria for selecting levels of protection are contained in chapter 2. Operational guidance (examples of) for inspections, exercising, tests, and accomplishing protection required is contained in the following publications and other applicable specifications and standards listed in the DODISS:

a. MCO P4030.31, Packaging of Materiel, Preservation (Volume I).

b. MIL-STD-105, Sampling Procedures and Tables for Inspection by Attributes.

c. MIL-P-116, Preservation, Methods of.

d. MIL-V-62038, Vehicle Wheeled, Preparation for Shipment and Storage of.

5005. <u>PRIORITY PROCESSING.</u> For effectiveness and efficiency of operations, priorities for reprocessing of technical items in storage (items requiring preservation/packing) should be established. Preference will be given to specific instructions which may be applicable to certain groups, categories, or types of items. Other priorities for reprocessing will be developed in consideration of the following criteria:

Priority	Explanation
1	serviceable material which will deteriorate to an unserviceable state if processing is deferred.
2	Material in support of known shipping demands.
3	Material administratively or physically earmarked for contingency plans.
4	Material received from depot maintenance.
5	New materiel received from procurement sources, the serviceability of which may be jeopardized by current status of preservation.
6	Other material in storage which is coded as serviceable, except for preservation required.
7	unserviceable, economically reparable materiel, pending repair action.

5006. <u>RECORDS OF INSPECTION AND REPROCESSING</u>

1. <u>Major Items (Operational Test Code (OTC) 1).</u> Records will be maintained to reflect the processing and reprocessing history for major end items of equipment and vehicles. Appropriate forms for annotating initial processing performed, inspection results, and reprocessing are prescribed in the documents listed in paragraph 5004, preceding, and may be supplemented, as deemed necessary by local instructions. Such records should provide for the accumulation of data which will indicate the reliability of specific packaging methods, materials, and processes. This data

will serve as a basis for adjustments in inspection/exercising cycles and updating of processing documents.

2. Secondary Items (OTC 2). Storage quality control records reflecting the packaging maintenance history for items other than those referred to in paragraph 5006.1, preceding, shall be maintained on form NAVMC 10579 (Care-in-Storage Inspection Record). A separate form shall be used for each line item inspected. The multiple copy set will facilitate work process planning, control, accountability, and movement of materiel to be reprocessed.

5007. IMPLEMENTING INSTRUCTIONS. Activity commanders shall issue inspections, as appropriate, implementing the procedures set forth herein, to ensure that all items are afforded adequate protection throughout the term of storage. Implementing instructions should also create an awareness throughout each command of the need for adequate protection to the extent that deficiencies in item protection will be noted (and corrective action taken) in conjunction with but not limited to the following:

1. Receiving operations.

2. Physical inventory.

3. Stock selection.

4. Preparation for shipment.

5. Care-in-storage.

MARINE CORPS PACKAGING MANUAL

CHAPTER 6

MARKING

MARINE CORPS PACKAGING MANUAL

CHAPTER 6

MARKING

6000. **GENERAL INFORMATION**

1. Proper markings are essential to assure positive identification
of preserved items and to facilitate efficient and effective
storage, issue, and inventory operations. Markings are applied
either to labels or directly to surfaces of barriers or containers.
In addition to item identity, markings give other necessary supply
management information concerning the item.

2. Inadequate/improper markings are considered to be the principal
cause of frustrated cargo at materiel receiving and supply
processing sites. Improper markings also cause excessive work-
hours to be devoted to technical research to establish proper
identification.

6001. **DEFINITION OF MARKING.** The application of numbers, letters,
labels, tags, symbols, or colors for handling or identification of
material during shipment and storage.

6002. **GUIDELINES**

1. Required markings will be complete, accurate, and legible.
Materials used for marking and methods of application will be per
the requirements of MIL-STD-129.

2. Standard markings for unit and intermediate packs include the
following:

    a. NSN.

    b. Item description.

    c. Quantity and unit of issue.

    d. Contract or purchase order number (when applicable) -

    e. Level of preservation and packing, and date.

3. Guidance concerning the placement of markings and labels for
unit and intermediate packs is contained in chapter 3, table 3-11
of MCO P4030.31C and MIL-STD-129. These procedures conform to the
requirement of MIL-P-116 for specified methods and submethods of
protection.

4. The color of all markings shall be black, except for applications to surfaces on which black would not be legible. The color used in those cases shall provide a distinct contrast with the surface to be marked.

5. Hand lettering of markings is not permitted, except as specified in MIL-STD-129.

6. Labels used for interior packs shall be printed, typed, or reproduced. The size of labels shall be consistent or proportionate with the size of the pack or surface for marking, and the size of lettering must permit ready identification. Labels for Level A shall be securely affixed with water-resistant label adhesive applied to the complete underside of the label. Paper labels for Level A, B, and C packs shall be waterproofed by coating the outer surface of the label with a waterproof lacquer, varnish, or acrylic coating compound.

7. The item manager sponsoring agency will ensure that specifications, standards, requests for procurement action, and contractual documents specify that markings for shipment and storage shall be per MIL-STD-129, unless otherwise specified.

6003. SPECIAL MARKINGS

1. Special and precautionary markings are often required to indicate peculiar characteristics of an item and/or method of preservation and to specify and facilitate proper handling. Examples include subsistence packs, shelf-life items, fragile items, ESDS items, hazardous material, method II preservation, etc. Requirements for special markings are detailed in MIL-STD-129.

2. Markings for packaged radioactive materiel shall be in accordance with MIL-STD-129.

3. Marking requirements and special handling data/certification for hazardous materials shipped by military aircraft are prescribed by MCO P4030.19.

6004. EXTERIOR MARKINGS

1. Markings applied to exterior containers, pallet loads, multipack containers, bales, bundles, or other configurations offered for shipment will be adequate to assure movement of the cargo without confusion and delay during shipment. Markings will also permit ready identification throughout the distribution cycle and facilitate proper handling.

2. Exterior markings will also conform to the applicable
provisions of DoD 4140.17-M and the DoD movement processing
regulation.

6005. <u>MIL-STD-129</u>. Previous paragraphs of this chapter bear out
the importance of adequate markings for interior and exterior packs
and should create an awareness for special markings that may be
required to facilitate proper storage, safety, and efficiency in
handling. MIL-STD-129 contains uniform requirements for marking
which are mandatory for use throughout the DoD. This standard is
the fundamental document for marking procedures and materials for
all classes of supply and will be followed in marking items for
storage and shipment.

MARINE CORPS PACKAGING MANUAL

CHAPTER 7

PACKAGING TRAINING

MARINE CORPS PACKAGING MANUAL

CHAPTER 7

PACKAGING TRAINING

7000. <u>GENERAL INFORMATION.</u> It is incumbent upon each activity having the responsibility for PP&P to ensure that all military and civilian personnel involved in PP&P are afforded training in military packaging. Included are personnel physically engaged in cleaning, preservation, packing, and marking operations; packaging inspection; and those involved in the preparation of packaging requirements to be incorporated in specifications, standards, and other technical and procurement documents.

7001. <u>TRAINING COURSES.</u> Resident training in military packaging is conducted at the School of Military Packaging Technology (SMPT), Aberdeen Proving Ground, Maryland. The following courses are offered (also see DoD 5010.16, Defense Management Education and Training Catalog):

1. Defense Preservation and Intermediate Protection, Course No. 8B-F1.

2. Defense Packing and Unitization, Course No. 8B-F2.

3. Defense Advanced Preservation and Packing, Course No. 8B-F3.

4. Defense Basic Preservation and Packing, Course No. 822-F13.

5. Defense Packaging Management Training Program, Course No. 8B-F26.

6. Defense Packaging Design, Course No. 8B-F16.

7. Defense Packaging of Hazardous Materials, Course No. 8B-F7.

8. Defense Packaging for Logistics Managers, Course No. 8B-F4.

9. Defense Foam-In-Place Packaging, Course No. 8B-F22 (JT).

10. Defense Packaging Data System, Course No. SMPT-4.

11. Packaging and Handling of Electrostatic Discharge Sensitive Items, Course No. SMPT-6.

12. Defense Vehicle Processing for Shipment or Storage, Course No. 8B-F6.

7002. <u>NONRESIDENT TRAINING</u>. The following correspondence courses are administered by SMPT:

1. Defense Preservation and Intermediate Protection, Course No. 8B-F1 (COR).

2. Defense Packing and Unitization, Course No. 8B-F2(COR)

3. Defense Marking for Shipment and Storage, Course No. 8B-F32 (COR).

4. Defense Preparation of Freight for Air Shipment, Course No. 8B-F36(COR).

5. Defense Basic Preservation and Packing, Course No. 822-F13(COR).

7003. <u>MOS TRAINING.</u> The training requirements for MOS 3052 commensurate with career progression are as follows:

1. <u>Entry Level (E-1 Through E-2)</u>.   Basic Packaging, Course No. SMPT-1 (MC).

2. <u>Career Level (E-3 Through E-6)</u>

    a. Defense Packaging of Hazardous Material for Transportation, Course No. 8B-F7/822-F7(JT).

    b. Defense Vehicle Processing for Shipment or Storage, Course No. 8B-F6/822-F6(JT).

    c. Defense (Refresher) Packaging of Hazardous Materials for Air Transportation, Course No. 8B-F35/822-F35(JT).

    d. Defense Preservation and Intermediate Protection, Course No. 8B-F1/822-F1(JT).

    e. Defense Packing and Unitization, Course No. 8B-F22/822-F2 (JT).

    f. Defense Foam-In-Place Packaging, Course No. 8B-F22/822-F22 (JT).

    g. Defense Packaging Data System, Course No. SMPT-4.

    h. Defense Marking for Shipment and Storage, Course No. 8B-F32(JT).

    i. Defense Advance Preservation and Packing, Course No. BB-F3(JT).

3. <u>Career Level (E-7 Through E-8)</u>

a. Defense Packaging Management Training Program, Course No. 8B-F26(JT).

b. Defense Packaging Design, Course No. 8B-F16(JT).

c. Defense Packaging for Logistics Managers Seminar, Course No. 8B-F4(JT).

d. Defense Packaging Instruction Training, Course No. 8B-F31/822-F31(JT).

7004. <u>ONSITE TRAINING.</u> SMPT also conducts onsite training in military packaging. Requests for information pertaining to onsite training should be submitted through local training activities. Onsite training is funded by the host activity.

7005. <u>LOCAL TRAINING</u>. Local training programs are essential for the development and maintenance of an effective packaging capability. OJT programs provide training for personnel who either do not meet the prerequisites for resident training at SMPT or have not had the opportunity to attend. OJT also serves as a means to keep personnel abreast of trends and developments in military packaging. Local training programs should be conducted by senior personnel who have completed the Defense Packaging Instructor Training Course. The following aids are recommended for use in local training programs:

1. MCO P4030.23 (Instructor's Guide for Basic Military Preservation and Packing).

2. MCO P4030.21 (course outline 8B-F2).

3. MCO P4030.31 (course outline 8B-F1).

4. Training films and videos.

7006. <u>AVAILABILITY OF TRAINING AIDS.</u> The directives listed in paragraph 7005.1, preceding, and other service indexes of publications are available through normal publication channels and are usually available in base libraries. Training films and videos are available at all DoD visual information centers. A listing of these materials may be found in DoD 5040.2-C-1 through DoD 5040.2-C-4, Catalog of Audiovisual Productions. Information concerning other technical publications and training aids which may be useful in local training may be obtained by contacting the CMC (LPP-2).

MARINE CORPS PACKAGING MANUAL

CHAPTER 8

PACKAGING DISCREPANCY REPORTING

MARINE CORPS PACKAGING MANUAL

CHAPTER 8

PACKAGING DISCREPANCY REPORTING

8000. <u>GENERAL INFORMATION.</u> Procedures are presented herein to provide for analysis of packaging throughout the Marine Corps distribution system and to establish procedures for the reporting of packaging discrepancies, excessive packaging, and recommendations for corrective action.

8001. <u>DEFINITION OF PACKAGING DISCREPANCY.</u> An unsatisfactory condition attributable to improper packaging. This includes any omission or misapplication of prescribed packaging requirements in specifications, standards, regulations, manuals, contracts, or packaging data sheets. These discrepancies apply to methods, materials, or procedures which cause or render the item, shipment, or package vulnerable to any loss, delay, or damage.

8002. <u>OBJECTIVE.</u> The Packaging Discrepancy Report Program is the basis of investigation into the quality of packaging accomplished (materials and workmanship). The primary objective is to determine causes of inadequate protection and avoid repetition of discrepancies which have already caused damage or could result in damage to Marine Corps materiel.

8003. <u>SCOPE AND-APPLICABILITY.</u> The procedures for reporting discrepancies in preservation, packing, unitization, marking, and handling are contained in MCO 4430.3 and are reportable on SF 364. These procedures are applicable to the reporting of all obvious or concealed defects, including damage attributable to inadequate preservation, packing, unitization, marking, handling, and excessive packaging. Shipments covered by these procedures may originate at a commercial vendor's facility, another Marine Corps installation, other military installations, or other Government agencies/activities.

8004. <u>REPORTABLE DISCREPANCIES</u>

1. Packaging discrepancies to be reported are defined in detail in SECNAVINST 4355.18, section VI. In order to attain maximum effectiveness, it is essential that all types of discrepancies enumerated in SECNAVINST 4355.18, section VI, be reported as they occur. Complete the SF 364 in its entirety, giving special attention to a detailed description of the discrepancy and actions taken or recommended to correct the discrepancy. Photographs, although not required, are very beneficial in support of the

discrepancy being reported. Photographs are also beneficial for the shipping activities use in evaluating the cause of the discrepancy and providing corrective action to prevent recurrence.

2. The types of discrepancies to be reported include the following:

    a. Discrepancies in item preparation, such as:

    (1) Corrosion.

    (2) Improper preservation (MIL-P-116).

    b. Inappropriate level of protection (when receipts are afforded protection at a level less than specified by contract or material release order).

    c. Wrong method of protection (MIL-P-116) and/or required materials; i.e., barriers, desiccant, and cushioning are missing, inadequate, or improperly used.

    d. Materials (and workmanship) do not meet contract requirements or do meet contract requirements but are inadequate.

    e. Inadequate protection for materiel in retrograde shipment (see chapter 9).

    f. Inadequate or improper cushioning, blocking, and bracing per MIL-STD-1186.

    g. Improper, inadequate, or incomplete marking (identification, address, certification, or special handling).

    h. Improper unitization/palletization.

3. The requirement for expeditious reporting of discrepancies which present a potential hazard to personnel, could impair military operations, and/or have an adverse affect on other material cannot be overemphasized. In these instances, the action prescribed in SECNAVINST 4355.18, section VI, paragraph A2b, will be taken.

4. DiscrepancieS in the preparation of dangerous materials for shipment by military aircraft warrant special attention. Applicable instructions are contained in MCO P4030.19.

8005. <u>DISTRIBUTION OF REPORTS</u>. Requirements for distribution of reports applicable to Marine Corps materiel are contained in SECNAVINST 4355.18, section VI, paragraph C. Reports of discrepancy shall be submitted to the COMMARCORLOGBASES, (Code 808-1), 814 Radford Boulevard, Albany, GA 31704-1128, for appropriate action, with a copy to the contracting activity.

8006. ACTION REQUIRED

1. All addressees shall immediately report all instances of obvious damage, or potential for damage, noted as a result of deficient preservation, packing, unitization, marking, and improper handling, per these instructions and the requirements of SECNAVINST 4355.18.

2. Activities receiving the action copy (original) of the SF 364 shall investigate the report, take corrective action, and inform the COMMARCORLOGBASES, (Code 808-1), Albany, by endorsement, of the action taken.

3. Unresolved ROD's will be forwarded by the screening point to the ROD's focal point, CMC (LPP-2), for assistance in bringing about a satisfactory resolution.

MARINE CORPS PACKAGING MANUAL

CHAPTER 9

FIELD EXPEDIENCIES AND PREPARATION OF RETROGRADE SHIPMENTS

MARINE CORPS PACKAGING MANUAL

CHAPTER 9

FIELD EXPEDIENCIES AND PREPARATION OF RETROGRADE SHIPMENTS

SECTION 1: EXPEDIENCIES IN PRESERVATION AND PACKING

9100. <u>GENERAL INFORMATION</u>

1. Many Marine Corps activities in some CONUS and overseas areas lack the capability to effectively perform preservation and packing. Notwithstanding, most activities have materiel in their custody for a considerable length of time for which proper care must be given and, as necessary, represerved.

2. Unserviceable reparable assets to be evacuated to maintenance sources are also of prime concern. These assets must be accorded protection to prevent deterioration to a state of being uneconomical to repair. Adequate protection must also be afforded excess material being returned to stores.

9101. <u>PURPOSE AND SCOPE.</u> To establish procedures for preservation and packing of unserviceable reparable materiel being evacuated to repair facilities, serviceable reparable-type items being returned as activity or command excess, and activity or command excess serviceable nonreparable-type items being returned to supply elements or to the stores system (see section 2 of this chapter); and to prescribe improvised procedures for accomplishing preservation and packing (see section 3 of this chapter) -

9102. <u>GUIDELINES</u>

1. Consistent with command capability and the availability of required materials and equipment, protection will be applied to all material being evacuated to repair facilities and/or supply support elements.

2. Prior to or in conjunction with preparing materiel for shipment, a limited technical inspection shall be performed on the following categories of equipment (see MCO P4400.82F, chapters 5 and 6):

    a. Major ordnance end items.

    b. Major motor transport end items.

    c. Major engineer end items.

    d. All class II, type I communication-electronics items.

    e. All class VII, type I communication-electronics items.

3. When all actions required by this Manual and shipment instructions peculiar to the equipment itself have been taken to prepare the equipment for shipment, the following certificate shall be accomplished and signed by the proper authority: "I certify that this equipment has been prepared for shipment per MCO P4030.36 and/or other applicable regulations." The certification shall be made on the applicable limited technical inspection form or affixed to it. This certificate, and a copy of the limited technical inspection form, shall accompany the equipment. Each organization receiving equipment for transfer, evacuation, or shipment shall verify its condition against the inspection form. When the capability of an organization limits the preparation to that set forth in section 3 of this chapter, the receiving activity shall be notified prior to shipment to facilitate processing of the item(s) upon receipt. Notification shall include the following:

    a. Item identification (noun nomenclature and NSN) -

    b. Anticipated date of shipment.

    c. Estimated date of arrival at the receiving activity.

    d. Mode of transportation and Government bill of lading number.

4. Compliance with-applicable instructions pertaining to decontamination of equipment and containers, and pest and rodent control are of prime importance for personnel safety and the prevention of the importation of disease to the United States.

5. Department of the Army Technical Manual TM 746-10 (General Packaging Instructions for Field Units) contains valuable information applicable to the preservation and packing of all classes of serviceable materiel for retrograde shipment. TM 746-10 also includes criteria for quarantine inspection and appendices that list packaging materials and equipment required for processing material. TM 746-10 is authorized for use by Marine Corps activities for guidance, and it can be obtained through normal publication channels.

MARINE CORPS PACKAGING MANUAL

CHAPTER 9

FIELD EXPEDIENCIES AND PREPARATION OF RETROGRADE SHIPMENTS

SECTION 2: PRESERVATION-PACKING EVACUATED ITEMS OF EQUIPMENT

9200. <u>GENERAL INSTRUCTIONS</u>

1. Prior to any preservation or packing effort, the item to be processed should be cleaned of mud, dirt, debris, and other foreign matter both inside and outside. Openings into the interior of vehicles or vehicle components should be sealed with barrier material and/or taped, or by other material suitable to prevent the entry of water, rodents, etc. Rusted surface areas normally protected by pain should be cleaned and spot-painted with any available paint or primer.

2. MCO P4030.31 and item packaging specifications and standards for processing specific items should be used as guides in accomplishing cleaning and preservation/packing of items being evacuated. Instructions for fabricating boxes and crates for boxed shipments are contained in MCO P4030.21.

3. MCO P4030.21, MCO P4030.31, and packaging process documents give preference to cleaning and preservation/packing materials which are manufactured for this purpose and conform to Federal and military specifications. Efforts should be made to obtain these materials through normal supply channels and to utilize them in affording protection to recoverable assets. In the absence of preferred materials or in conjunction therewith, prudence will dictate the use of substitute materials recommended in section 3 of this chapter.

9201. <u>MOTOR TRANSPORT EQUIPMENT</u>

1. Particular attention shall be given to the protection of assemblies, subassemblies, and components. They should be complete and assembled to the degree possible prior to packing.

2. Vehicles, assemblies, subassemblies, and components which are in Condition Code A, B, or C will be preserved and packed per the instructions contained in the operator and organizational maintenance manual or the item specification, if available.

3. Vehicles, assemblies, subassemblies, and components which are being returned to stock in Condition Code D through Z shall be preserved and packed, to the degree necessary (minimum protection), to prevent further deterioration and physical damage during shipment and/or storage pending repair.

4. All collateral equipment should be packaged per the instructions contained in the operators and organizational maintenance manual for the item or the specification which applies to the equipment, if available, and secured to the vehicle in a manner to prevent pilferage and loss.

9202. <u>ELECTRICAL/ELECTRONIC EQUIPMENT, VEHICULAR-MOUNTED</u>

1. Mounted equipment which is in Condition Code A, B, or C should be preserved per the instructions contained in the operations and organizational maintenance manual or the item specification, if available.

2. Electrical/electronic equipment in Condition Code D through Z, which requires inspection and repair prior to return to stock, should be protected to the degree necessary to prevent further corrosion and/or damage while in transit or awaiting inspection and/or repair.

3. The vehicle on which the electrical/electronic equipment is mounted will be protected per the instructions contained in paragraph 9201, preceding.

9203. <u>ELECTRICAL AND ELECTRONIC EQUIPMENT, UNMOUNTED.</u> Electronic equipment which is not mounted on a vehicle should be protected per the instructions contained in paragraph 9202, preceding.

9204. <u>ORDNANCE EQUIPMENT (SELF-PROPELLED AND TOWED)</u>

1. In addition to the instructions contained in the operators and organizational maintenance manual, the following packaging instructions apply to ordnance equipment in Condition Code A, B, or C:

    a. The basic vehicle and vehicle accessories should be cleaned, lubricated, and preserved as specified for motor transport equipment in paragraph 9201, preceding.

    b. Communication equipment should be treated as specified for electronic equipment in paragraph 9202, preceding.

    c. Ordnance equipment which requires repair prior to return to storage should be protected to the degree necessary to prevent further corrosion and/or damage while in transit or awaiting repair.

d. Polished metal surfaces and matting surfaces shall be cleaned to remove all corrosion and contaminates; then, coated with the appropriate preservative and wrapped with a greaseproof, waterproof barrier material.

e. Gun tube bores shall be cleaned with a solvent which will dissolve powder residue and remove corrosion and contaminates. After cleaning, the bores shall be coated with type P-9 preservative; and a volatile corrosion inhibitor treated tube shall be placed inside the gun tube and plugged. The plug shall be sealed in the bore with waterproof, greaseproof tape conforming to PPP-T-60 or equal.

f. Equipment which is normally removed for shipment should be packaged per the specification or other applicable documents. It should then be attached to the equipment in such a manner as to discourage pilferage and prevent loss while in transit.

g. Lenses of optical equipment (vision blocks) should be wiped clean with surgical cotton or lens tissue to remove contamination. The lenses should then be covered with cotton or lens tissue secured with PPP-T-76 tape, cushioned with PPP-C-1797 cushioning material secured with PPP-T-76, further protected by unit padding in a MIL-B-131 barrier bag, and then packed in a PPP-B-636 fiberboard container.

2. Ordnance equipment in Condition Code D through Z, which requires inspection and repair prior to return to stock, will be packaged to the degree necessary to prevent further corrosion and/or damage while in transit and/or storage pending repair.

9205. SHELTER (VAN) MOUNTED EQUIPMENT. In addition to the instructions in the operators and organizational maintenance manual and the item specification, the following packing instructions apply to shelter-mounted equipment in Condition Code A, B, and C:

1. Empty space in drawers or cabinets partially filled with tools or test equipment should be filled with cushioning material, such as rubberized hair, shredded paper, etc. Reclaimed cushioning materials may be used for this purpose. Latches or drawer catches should be securely fastened and safety-wired, when applicable. All heavy items should be removed from drawers/cabinets and packaged separately and properly secured within the shelter.

2. Mounted electronic components require special handling. Electron tube hold-down clamps shall be secured in place. Module hold-down screws should be checked for tightness. Shock mounts, when used, should be inspected for condition, completeness of mounting screws, and tightness. Strapping should be applied to suspended equipment. Mounting racks shall be inspected for

tightness and completeness of mounting bolts or retainers. Floor-stowed material should be strapped or bolted in place. Crush skids shall be inspected prior to shipment. If damaged, wooden skids shall be strapped in place to serve as dunnage and to prevent additional damage.

3. Matting surfaces and machined surfaces on the exterior of the shelter shall be cleaned of all contamination and coated with the appropriate preservative; then, covered with waterproof, greaseproof barrier material secured with waterproof, greaseproof PPP-T-60 tape.

4. Shelter doors shall be securely fastened and safety-wired through the locking hasp. Wide waterproof tape shall be used to seal all doors, ports, windows, power entrances, and cable entrances to prevent the entry of water or other contaminants.

5. Items in Condition Code D through Z shall be processed to the degree necessary to prevent further deterioration or damage while in transit or awaiting repair.

9206. <u>GENERAL PROPERTY EQUIPMENT (SELF-PROPELLED AND TOWED) IN CONDITION CODE A, B, OR C.</u> The basic vehicle should be processed per the instructions contained in paragraph 9201, preceding. On-vehicle equipment, such as truck-mounted firefighting equipment, valves, and nozzles, should be drained of water and sealed against the entry of moisture and dirt. Pumping systems should be flushed with type P-3 preservative.

9207. <u>MARKING</u>. In addition to the marking instructions contained in chapter 6, the following special markings are required:

1. Appropriate warning labels will be attached in conspicuous places, such as the operator's compartments, as precautionary measures to prevent damage to equipment or injury to personnel.

2. Warning labels will contain instructions as to what depreservation steps must be taken prior to operation. They may also contain information regarding any unusual measures taken in the preservation cycle (such as overfilling the crankcases of engines) and instructions on methods for removing the preservation materials.

9208. <u>PROCESSING CRITERIA.</u> In addition to the general instructions set forth in paragraphs 9200 through 9207, preceding, the following documents are representative of specifications containing detailed processing criteria for major items of self-propelled equipment, skid-mounted powered equipment, and secondary technical items:

1. MIL-V-62038, Vehicle, Wheeled, Preparation for Shipment and Storage of.

2. MIL-E-10062, Engine, Preparation for Shipment and Storage of.

3. MIL-E-17555, Electronic and Electrical Equipment, Accessories, and Repair Parts, Packaging and Packing of.

4. MIL-T-45309, Tank, Combat, Full-Tracked, 105mm Gun, M60 and M60A1, Processing for Shipment and Storage of.

5. MIL-T-62340, Tank, Combat, Full-Tracked, M1 Series, Processing for Shipment and Storage of.

CHAPTER 9

FIELD EXPEDIENCIES AND PREPARATION OF RETROGRADE SHIPMENTS

SECTION 3: FIELD EXPEDIENCIES IN PRESERVATION AND PACKING

9300. <u>GENERAL INFORMATION.</u> Field expediencies, as related to packaging, are any processes wherein the using unit prepares material for shipment to another location using improvised equipment and methods. It is not implied that improvised preservation methods will meet the workmanship and performance requirements of specifications for the packaging of new equipment. Nevertheless, field applied preservation will serve to maintain the material in the same condition as when shipped.

9301. <u>DISASSEMBLY AND MATCH MARKING.</u> When it becomes necessary to disassemble equipment for shipment, all nuts, bolts, screws, pins, etc., shall be cleaned, preserved, bagged, and attached to the mating parts. All mating parts shall be marked in such a manner that they may be easily reassembled.

9302. <u>CLEANING PROCESS.</u> Rust should be removed from all items prior to applying a preservative coating or packing. This can be accomplished by portable sanders or sanding by hand, scraping, or the use of impact tools. Contaminants, such as accumulated road dirt, mud, and grease, should be removed by steam-cleaning and by solvents. Recommended substitute solvents are paint thinners, diesel fuel, alcohol, and hot water.

9303. <u>RINSING.</u> After the item has been cleaned, the next step is rinsing. This is done in another tank or receptacle containing clean solvent of the same kind used in the cleaning operation or hot water, depending on the method and cleaning materials used. The solvent or water used for rinsing should be changed frequently to maintain it as clean as possible and to avoid too much contamination due to carryover from the cleaning tank.

9304. <u>DRYING.</u> Several methods of drying, which can be employed in the field, are prepared compressed air, ovens, spotlights, and ordinary light bulbs. If none of these methods are available, drain and wipe with clean, dry cloths. It is important that the items not be contaminated by handling or exposure to contaminants after they have been cleaned and dried.

9305. <u>APPLICATION OF PRESERVATIVES.</u> Preservative coatings, when required, should be applied as soon as possible after drying. If the preservatives specified by MCO P4030.31 and MIL-P-116 are available, type P-1 preservative will be adequate for most noncritical surfaces. Types P-9, P-10, and P-11 preservatives may be used for most machined surfaces. If the aforementioned P-type preservatives are unavailable, normal operating oils and greases will be used.

9306. <u>FIELD-CONSTRUCTED EQUIPMENT</u>

1. The following applies to field-constructed equipment:

    a. <u>Hot-Dip Tank.</u> A hot-dip tank may be constructed by cutting a 55-gallon drum (girthwise) to make a round tank and adding a heating element from a range unit or other improvised manner.

    b. <u>Cold-Solvent Tank.</u> A cold-solvent tank may be constructed by cutting a 55-gallon drum lengthwise and placing it on stands. A cover should be made to fit the tank as tightly as possible.

    c. <u>Drying Oven.</u> A drying oven may be constructed from a 55-gallon drum with the gasoline heating element from a field kitchen stove used to supply the heat required.

    d. <u>Hot Water and Alkaline Cleaning Tank.</u> A 55-gallon drum, with the top removed to make a vat, may be used as a hot water or an alkaline cleaning tank. Steam from a steam-cleaning unit may be used to provide the heat, and kitchen lye may be used as an alkaline cleaning material.

    e. <u>Small Parts Dipping Baskets.</u> Small parts dipping baskets may be constructed from cans with holes punched in the sides and bottom so as not to trap solvent. A wire bail should be attached for handling of the baskets. Cans of various sizes may be obtained from the dining facility. These baskets can also be made from screen wire, hardware, or cloth.

    f. <u>Two-Compartment Container for Engine Preservation.</u> The two-compartment container required to process the engine can be fabricated from two 5-gallon military-designed gas cans banded together. Suitable connections and flexible tubing connected to each container coupled into a single line by a regulator valve and a quick-disconnect coupling at the end of the single line will complete the assembly. One compartment shall be clearly marked "fuel" and the other marked "oil."

2. Buildings where packaging operations are performed shall be well ventilated and the areas well marked. Firefighting equipment should be provided, and all personnel involved in the packaging

operations instructed on its use. The firefighting equipment shall be easily accessible and its location well marked.

3. Outside areas that are set aside for packaging operations shall be well marked. Signs shall be located in such a manner as to warn personnel of the hazards within the area. Firefighting equipment shall be located within the area, and all personnel who are involved in the packaging operation shall be instructed in its use and location. Care should be taken to prevent the spillage of solvents within the area, thereby avoiding a fire hazard.

4. The packaging operation should be located near an area where materials can be protected from pilferage and contamination. It is desirable to locate the packaging facility as near the shipping point as possible to prevent recontamination of the material and to avoid unnecessary handling.

5. Personnel should be cautioned against smoking or carrying an open flame in areas where flammable materials are used or stored. Personnel should also be instructed to use proper protective clothing (gloves, goggles, aprons, and breathing masks, as appropriate) for protection against skin irritations and the possible toxic/allergic affects of cleaning and preserving materials.

9307. <u>SALVAGE OF MATERIALS.</u> Packaging materials can often be salvaged from material receipts and reused for shipments. Care must be taken during the opening of a container and removal of the contents to preserve the packaging materials as much as possible. These materials may be reused to wrap, cushion, package, and pack unserviceable reparable items for return shipment. Examples of materials which can be salvaged and reused are as follows:

1. Barrier materials.

2. Cushioning materials.

3. Wood cleated fiberboard containers.

4. Metal and plastic containers.

5. Fiberboard die cuts and wood blocking and bracing.

6. Wooden containers.

7. Fiberboard containers (singlewall, doublewall, triplewall, and fastpack containers)

9308. <u>INTERIOR CONTAINERS.</u> Any small container(s) available shall serve to segregate fragile items from other material or to keep the parts of a disassembled item together. Containers may be made from salvaged fiberboard material, cut to the appropriate size, and fastened at the joints with wire or tape. Salvaged canvas barracks bags, discarded tarps, etc., may be used to contain items within the container.

9309. <u>CUSHIONING</u>

1. Cushioning is an essential part of packaging. Items must be cushioned within the unit package and cushioned again when the unit packages are packed into consolidation containers. Reclaimed cushioning materials may be used to protect the items from damage caused by environments within the container. The cushioning material should be dry and noncorrosive. Items which are coated with a preservative should be wrapped with a greaseproof barrier material. Space between the item and the interior of the container must be sufficient to allow for cushioning, as necessary to protect the item.

2. Articles which do not completely fill the unit container should be blocked, braced, fastened, or otherwise secured within the container. Items having protruding parts which may be broken or may puncture the container or barrier should be supported or suspended and cushioned.

9310. <u>CONSOLIDATION CONTAINERS</u>. A savings in space and handling can be realized by the use of containers to consolidate items. Containers may be those in which shipments were received or may be fabricated from materials on hand. Care should be taken to ensure that the items within are immobilized, by use of blocking and bracing or cushioning. Weight of the containers (contents) should be limited to that which will facilitate handling and not overload containers.

9311. <u>REUSABLE CONTAINERS.</u> Materiel returned to overhaul rebuild points (logistics bases or contractor facilities) will, whenever possible, be shipped in the reusable container in which the item was received. Use of the designed container is required, if available, since the interior is specifically designed to permit easy repositioning of the failed item and provides necessary blocking, bracing, and cushioning.

9312. <u>MARKING.</u> All packages and exterior containers shall be afforded proper identification and shipment markings. Marking instructions are contained in MIL-STD-129 and chapter 6 of this Manual. In the absence of required marking materials (stencil boards and waterproof marking inks), marking shall be applied by use of paints and shall be legible.

MARINE CORPS PACKAGING MANUAL

CHAPTER 10

PACKAGING REFERENCES

MARINE CORPS PACKAGING MANUAL

CHAPTER 10

PACKAGING REFERENCES

10000. <u>GENERAL INFORMATION</u>. The references in this chapter are a partial listing of basic packaging documents (technical, administrative, operational, training, and procedural in nature) and are presented here as a ready reference. The listing will prove helpful to personnel involved in other elements of supply and distribution on which packaging has an impact or interface (i.e., procurement, technical, stock management, transportation, storage, and warehousing).

10001. <u>AVAILABILITY OF REFERENCES</u>. Activity allowances have been established for only a limited number of the publications listed in this chapter. It is recognized that the limited distribution allowance may not be adequate and that many activities now engaged in PP&P are not covered by established distribution allowances. Nevertheless, these and other publications, as may be listed in

DoD 4120.3-M and other services indexes, are available as follows:

1. Military Specifications and Standards. Refer to MCO 4120.5.

2. Marine Corps Letter and P-Type Directives and Joint Services Publications. Refer to MCO P5600.31G, section III.

3. Other Services Publications. Refer to MCO P5600.31G, section III.

10002. <u>LIST OF PACKAGING REFERENCES</u>. It is emphasized that the following listing of packaging publications is limited to basic documents covering commonly used materials and containers, DoD-approved methods of preservation and packing, technical and procedural documents covering the packaging of "groups" of items of similar characteristics, and documents setting forth care and preservation procedures for "types" of equipment.

<u>1. Marine Cords Letter and "P" Type Directives</u>

<u>MCO Number</u>	<u>Subject</u>
4000.51	Logistics Application of Automated Marking and Reading Symbols
4030.16	Packaging and Packaging Maintenance of Small Arms Weapons, Using Volatile Corrosion Inhibitor (VCI) Treated Materials

MCO Number	Subject
P4030.19	Packaging and Materials Handling, Preparing Hazardous Materials for Military Air Shipment
P4030.21	Packaging of Material, Packing (Volume II)
P4030.23	Instructor's Guide for Basic Military Preservation and Packing
P4030.24	Logistics-Packaging Management
P4030.30	Preparation of Freight for Air Shipment
P4030.31	Packaging of Materiel, Preservation (Volume I)
4030.33	Packaging of Material
4030.34	Lead Activities for Testing Packaging Materials and Processes
4030.40	Packaging of Hazardous Materials
P4400.105	Radioactive Commodities in the DoD Supply System
P4450.7	Marine Corps Warehousing Manual
4870.62	Preparation of Industrial Plant Equipment for Storage or Shipment
5100.8	Marine Corps Ground Occupational Safety and Health (OSH) Program
5420.17	Marine Corps Preservation, Packaging, and Packing (P3) Committee

2. Military Specifications

Identification Number	Subject
MIL-E-75	Electron Tubes, Packaging of
MIL-P-116	Preservation, Methods of
MIL-B-117	Bag, Sleeves and Tubing - Interior Packaging
MIL-B-121	Barrier Material, Greaseproofed, Waterproofed, Flexible

Identification Number	Subject
MIL-P-130	Paper, Wrapping, Laminated and Creped
MIL-B-131	Barrier Materials, Water Vaporproofed, Flexible, Heat-Sealable
MIL-R-196	Repair Parts, Accessories and Kits, Mechanical, Packaging of
MIL-B-197	Bearings, Antifriction; Associated Parts and Subassemblies; Preparation for Delivery of
MIL-B-208	Battery, Storage, Lead Acid, Automotive and Navy, Portable (Except Aircraft), Packaging and Packing of
MIL-G-762	Grader, Road, Packaging of
MIL-R-3075	Rollers, Motorized, Road, Diesel or Gasoline-Engine Driven, Packaging of
MIL-T-3351	Tractor, Full Tracked, Low Speed, Tractor, Wheeled, Agriculture and Tractor, Wheeled, Industrial, and Their Attachments, Packaging of
MIL-P-3420	Packaging Material, Volatile Corrosion Inhibitor, Treated, Opaque
MIL-C-3580	Crane and Crane-Shovels, Truck, Crawler, and Wheel Mounted, Full Revolving, and Their Attachments, Packaging of
MIL-I-8574	Inhibitors, Corrosion, Volatile, Utilization of
MIL-E-10062	Engine, Preparation for Shipment and Storage of
MIL-L-10547	Liner, Case, and Sheet, Overwrap, Water Vaporproof or Waterproof, Flexible
MIL-C-11264	Crates, Wood, Vehicular Assemblies, Reusable Shipping Containers for Tank-Automotive engines, Transmissions, Differentials, Transfers, Final Drives, and Similar Assemblies

Identification Number	Subject
MIL-B-12841	Basic Issue Items for Military Vehicles, Carriages and Equipment, Preparation for Shipment and Storage of
MIL-C-14200	Container, Shipping and Storage, Metal, Reusable, for Engines, Transmissions, Differentials, Transfers, and Similar Assemblies
MIL-P-14232	Parts, Equipment and Tools for Army Material, Packaging of
MIL-P-14313	Pistols and Revolvers, Packaging of
MIL-E-16298	Machines, Electric, Having Rotating Parts and Associated Repair Parts, Packaging of
MIL-E-17555	Electronic and Electrical Equipment Accessories, and Provisioned Items (Repair Parts), Packaging of
MIL-B-17757	Boxes, Shipping, Fiberboard (Modular Sizes)
MIL-L-21260	Lubricating Oil, Internal Combustion Engine, Preservative and Break-in
MIL-B-22019	Barrier Materials, Transparent, Flexible, Sealable, Volatile Corrosion Inhibitor Treated
MIL-B-22020	Bag, Transparent, Flexible, Sealable, Volatile Corrosion Inhibitor Treated
MIL-T-22085	Tape, Pressure-Sensitive Adhesive, Preservation and Sealing
MIL-B-22191	Barrier Materials, Transparent, Flexible, Heat Sealable
MIL-B-26195	Boxes, Wood-Cleated, skidded, Load-Bearing Base
MIL-B-40028	Bags, Barrier, With Volatile Corrosion Inhibitor Treated Liners
MIL-B-43666	Boxes, Shipping, Consolidation

Identification Number	Sublet
MIL-T-45309	Tank, Combat, Full-Tracked, 105mm Gun: M60, M60A1, M60A1(RISE), and M60A3; Processing for Shipment and Storage of
MIL-P-46002	Preservative Oil, Contact, and Volatile Corrosion Inhibited
MIL-V-62038	Vehicles, Wheeled: Preparation for Shipment and Storage of
MIL-T-62340	Tank, Combat, Full-Tracked, M1 Series, Processing for Shipment and Storage of

3. Military Standards

Identification Number	Subject
MIL-STD-101	Color Code for Pipelines and for Compressed Gas Cylinders
MIL-STD-105	Sampling Procedures and Tables for Inspection by Attributes
MIL-STD-129	Marking for Shipment and Storage
MIL-STD-129-1	Marking for Shipment and Storage Ammunition and Explosives
MIL-STD-129-2	Marking for Shipment and Storage Medical Material
MIL-STD-129-3	Marking for Shipment and Storage - Semiperishable and Perishable Subsistence
MIL-STD-147	Palletized Unit Loads
MIL-STD-162	Materials Handling Equipment: Preparation for Shipment, Storage, Cyclic Maintenance Routine Testing and Processing
MIL-STD-212	Preparation of Household Goods and Unaccompanied Baggage for Shipment, Storage, Intra-City, and Intra-Area Movements

Identification Number	Subject
MIL-STD-281	Automobiles, Trucks, Truck-Tractors, Trailers, and Trailer Dollies; Preservation and Packaging of
MIL-STD-290	Packaging of Petroleum and Related Products
MIL-STD-1186	Cushioning, Anchoring, Bracing, Blocking, and Waterproofing, With Appropriate Test Methods
MIL-STD-1187	Standard Size Unit, Intermediate and Exterior Containers for Modular Packaging and Unitization on the 40 Inch by 48 Inch Pallet
MIL-STD-1189	Standard Department of Defense Bar Code Symbology
MIL-STD-1367	Packaging, Handling, Storage, and Transportability (PHS&T) Program Requirements (for Systems and Equipment)
MIL-STD-1510	Container Design Retrieval System, Procedures for Use of
MIL-STD-1686	Electrostatic Discharge Control Program for Protection of Electrical and Electronic Parts, Assemblies and Equipment (excluding Electrically Initiated Explosive Devices) Metric
MIL-STD-2073-1	DoD Material Procedures For Development and Application of Packaging Requirements
MIL-STD-2073-2	Packaging Requirement Codes

4. Federal standards

Identification Number	Subject
FED-STD-101	Test Procedures for Packaging Materials

5. Federal Specifications

Identification Number	Subject
P-D-680	Dry Cleaning Solvent
UU-T-625	Stencilboard
UU-T-81	Tags, Shipping and Stock
MMM-A-250	Adhesive, Water-Resistant (for Closure of Fiberboard Boxes)
MMM-A-260	Adhesive, Water-Resistant (for Sealing Waterproof Paper)
PPP-B-601	Boxes, Wood, Cleated-Plywood
PPP-B-621	Boxes, Wood, Nailed and Lock Corner
PPP-B-636	Boxes, Shipping, Fiberboard
PPP-B-665	Boxes, Paperboard, Metal Edged and Components
PPP-B-1055	Barrier Material, Waterproofed, Flexible
PPP-B-1672	Box, Shipping, Reusable with Cushioning
PPP-C-843	Cushioning Material, Cellulosic
PPP-C-1797	Cushioning Material, Resilient, Low Density, Unicellular, Polypropylene Foam
PPP-P-40	Packaging and Packing of Hand Tools
PPP-T-60	Tape, Packaging, Waterproof
PPP-T-76	Tape, Packaging, Paper (for Carton Sealing)

6. Other Service Publications

Identification Number	Subject
AMCP 706-121	Engineering Design Handbook, Packaging and Pack Engineering

Identification Number	Subject
TM 746-10	General Packaging Instructions for Field Units

7. Military Handbooks

Identification Number	Subject
MIL-HDBK-263	Electrostatic Discharge Control Program for Protection of Electronic Parts, Assemblies and Equipment (excluding Electrically Initiated Explosive Devices) Metric
MIL-HDBK-304	Package Cushioning Design
MIL-HDBK-742	Waste Disposal for Military Packaging Materials
MIL-HDBK-770	Shrink Film/Stretch Wrap in Military Packaging
MIL-HDBK-773	Electrostatic Discharge Protective Packaging

8. Commercial Industry Standards

Identification Number	Subject
ASTM D 3950	Specification for Strapping, Nonmetallic (and Joining Methods)
ASTM D 3951	Practice for Commercial Packaging
ASTM D 3953	Specification for Strapping, Flat Steel and Seals

APPENDIX A

ABBREVIATIONS AND ACRONYMS

AMCP	Army Material Command Pamphlet
CCP	Consolidation/Containerization Point
CMC	Commandant of the Marine Corps
COMMARCORLOGBASES	Commander, Marine Corps Logistics Bases
CONUS	Continental United States
DIDS	Defense Integrated Data System
DoD	Department of Defense
DPPG	Defense Packaging Policy Group
DSSC	Direct Support Stock Control
ESD	Electrostatic Discharge
ESDS	Electrostatic Discharge Sensitive
FMF	Fleet Marine Force
FMS	Foreign Military Sales
FSSG	Force Service Support Group
ICAO	International Civil Air Organization
IL	International Logistics
IMDG	International Maritime Dangerous Goods
LOGMARS	Logistics Application of Automated Marking and Reading Symbols
MAGTF	Marine Air-Ground Task Force
MTMC	Military Traffic Management Command
MAP	Military Assistance Program
MOS	Military Occupational Specialty
NSN	National Stock Number

MARINE CORPS PACKAGING MANUAL

OCONUS	Outside of CONUS
OJT	On-the-Job Training
OSH	Occupational Safety and Health
OTC	Operational Test Code
PP&P	Preservation, Packaging, and Packing
POP	Performance Oriented Packaging
PWRS	Prepositioned War Reserve Stock
ROD	Report of Discrepancy
SMPT	School of Military Packaging Technology
UN	United Nations
VCI	Volatile Corrosion Inhibitor

A-2